# G[illegible]ines to Effective Personal Bible Study

FAITH A. OYEDEPO

**Guidelines To Effective Personal Bible Study**



**Faith A. Oyedepo**

ISBN 978-978-2480-25-5

Reprint: 2018, 2022, 2023

*Published in Nigeria by:*

**DOMINION PUBLISHING HOUSE**



*For further information or permission, address:*
**DOMINION PUBLISHING HOUSE**
Km 10, Idiroko Road, Canaanland, Ota, Nigeria.
Tel: +234 816 406 0777, +234 909 151 4022

Or visit our website: ***www.dphprints.com***

***Connect with Faith A. Oyedepo***

Faith Abiola Oyedepo

@faithoyedepo

@officialfaithoyedepo

*www.faithoyedepo.org*

*All Scripture quotations are from the King James Version of the Bible, except otherwise stated.*

# CONTENTS

Introduction 5

**Chapter 1**

The Bible 11

**Chapter 2**

Study Methods 25

**Chapter 3**

Study Tools 43

**Chapter 4**

Study Steps 49

**Chapter 5**

Benefits of Studying the Bible 61

**Chapter 6**

Covenant Platforms 71

**Chapter 7**

The Place of Prayer and Fasting 79

**Chapter 8**

The Principal Teacher: The Holy Spirit 85

**Chapter 9**

Maximising the Benefits of the Word 105

# Introduction

***Thy word is a lamp unto my feet, and a light unto my path.***

*Psalm 119:105*

As Christians, we are often encouraged to study the Word of God daily. To some, it is a religious requirement; so, they feel a sense of guilt if they do not read it daily. To others, they do not even bother to read it, until perhaps they get to church and are required to open their Bibles.

To another group, it is a very complex storybook that chronicles the life history of the ancient people of God. So, they read and see the stories as relating only to others.

To yet another, it is just so difficult to get into the routine of daily Word study, because of their very busy schedule.

Why is this so? A man of wisdom said, "When purpose is not known, abuse is inevitable."

The Bible is neither a religious book nor a book of "dos and don'ts". It is the foundation of our belief in God. It is about a relationship with a person – Jesus, the Word of God. It is a manual that has all the information you need, for correct and optimal relationship with Jesus.

2 Timothy 3:16-17 (ESV) says:

***All Scripture is breathed out by God and profitable for teaching, for reproof, for correction, and for training in righteousness, that the man of God***

> ***may be competent, equipped for every good work.***

It is a manual that equips you for good works. As God's divinely-inspired Word, the Bible offers us God's forgiveness for our sins and proffers solutions to the weights (issues of life) that easily beset us. It reveals His purpose for our lives and shows us His perspective on how we can live peaceably in a world of disorder.

Besides, it gives us directions on how to appropriate His power and how to be profitable witnesses for Him.

All that God requires of you is:

> ***As newborn babes, desire the sincere milk of the word, that ye may grow thereby.***
>
> *1 Peter 2:2*

Daily growth is a major focus of Word study. Making out time to study the Word daily, will grant you access to the power in it that will transform you into the person God wants you to be. Once you engage in Word study, you will experience the joy and peace required to enjoy life daily.

Personally, I have derived so much joy in discovering biblical truths through Word study. They are pillars that have ruled, guided and defended my life in all situations and circumstances of life.

However, as important as this subject is, getting started is the challenge with many believers. Having this book with you now is a unique opportunity. The truth is: There is no better "skill" than handling your Bible with good understanding and accuracy.

By the time you are through with this book, your Bible will become your daily companion, studying the Word will become your daily desire, and your Word study life will never remain the same!

# 1 The Bible

***All scripture is given by inspiration of God, and is profitable for doctrine, for reproof, for correction, for instruction in righteousness:***

***That the man of God may be perfect, thoroughly furnished unto all good works.***

*2 Timothy 3:16-17*

## What is the Bible?

This question is fundamental, in your quest for how to study the Bible. The Bible, which is interchangeably called the Word of God or the Holy Scripture, contains sacred writings.

What foundation is to a building is what the Word of God is to a believer. Every building indispensably depends on its foundation to stand. The Word of God is vital to a successful Christian life because it is the source of truth, the standard for a meaningful life, the revelation of Jesus Christ, the key to true liberty and the real food for man's soul.

Perhaps, a good understanding of the significance of the Bible, as distinct from any other book, will help you to appreciate its indispensability in your life as a Christian.

## The Bible is not an ordinary book

Just as with an effective use of a manual, you cannot go wrong with the use of a device; likewise, all that you require for a fruitful productive life is packaged in the Bible.

**It is a mystery book that gives us mastery over the affairs of life**
*(Hebrews 4:12)*

When you have an understanding of God's Word on any subject matter, you gain mastery in that area. For instance, if you understand the mystery of prosperity from studying the Word, your faith will come alive and you will become a master in that area.

The more you read and meditate daily on God's Word, the more mastery you gain over the issues of life that confront you.

The Bible is God's Word in print. It says:

***All Scripture is God-breathed and is useful for teaching, rebuking, correcting***

***and training in righteousness.***

*2 Timothy 3:16 (NIV)*

The Bible is God-breathed as God revealed the truth about Himself to holy men and inspired them to record every sentence, word and line in perfect agreement with His will.

The Bible, even though written by about 40 men of several backgrounds over a period of about 1,500 years, has one unified great theme and central figure – Jesus Christ. An aspect of His ministry is, establishing God's plan for salvation by providing deliverance from sin and spiritual death through repentance and faith. This would have been impossible if it was not inspired by one supreme Author – the Holy Spirit.

For instance, in the book of Genesis,

Moses graphically wrote about the events of creation as if he was a physical witness. David, a man after God's heart, spoke about what transpired even before the creation of the earth. The plan of redemption was unfolded to him by the inspiration of the Almighty. So, the Bible is not to be taken on the surface level. It is God's Word in print for your profiting.

Furthermore, the Bible can be seen as God's love letter to you. It tells of God's great compassion for you, and His desire to have fellowship with you.

### It is the book of answers to all life's questions

*(Matthew 4:1-11)*

There is no issue of life that is not mentioned in the Bible. When you make some discoveries and apply the same principles to your life, you will obtain the same result.

When Jesus was tempted, He overcame by the revelation of the Word.

I remember a sister's testimony several years ago. Her husband used to wander away from home, for months, without any rational explanation. At a time, he left and never returned for about seven years. This lady came to our church and heard that the Bible has an answer to every question of life. So, she began to search the Scripture for her answer.

Starting from Genesis chapter one, she studied book after book, until she got to Jeremiah. There, she discovered the Word that pertained to her situation. She said a prayer of faith, based on the revelation of the truth she contacted from that Word; her husband returned home and this time, to stay.

**It is the carrier of God's power**
*(Romans 1:16; Hebrews 4:12)*

It has the ability to change your life, because there is power in the Word. When all medical helps failed, it was the power in the Word of God, as recorded in my book, *The Healing Scriptures,* that rescued me from the valley of the shadow of death as explained in my book, *Rescued From Destruction.*

**It is the spiritual meat for strength**
*(Hebrews 5:13-14; 1 Kings 19:7-15; John 4:32-34)*

The Word of God is indeed the spiritual meat that gives you strength, when it is needed the most. It infuses health and vitality in place of weakness; it gives you courage when you are utterly discouraged. The Word of God gives you satisfaction in unimaginable dimensions.

When you lay hold on the promises of God in your area of concern, the Word releases strength to hold on to Him assured that He never fails.

**It is the water of life for supernatural refreshment**

*(Isaiah 55:1, 11; Revelation 21:6, 22:17; John 4:13-14)*

There is a longing in the heart of every living soul that only the Word of God has the capacity to satisfy. The water of life you encounter as you study the Word brings you a refreshing the way cold water does to a thirsty soul.

**It is the spiritual wine for conquest** *(Isaiah 55:3, 11; Genesis 49:9-12; Philippians 1:27-28)*

The truth of God's Word you discover keeps you steadfast and unshakable in the battles of life, confident that you are coming out triumphant.

> ***Only let your conversation be as it becometh the gospel of Christ: that whether I come and see you, or else be absent, I may hear of your affairs, that ye stand fast in one spirit, with one mind striving together for the faith of the gospel;***
>
> ***And in nothing terrified by your adversaries: which is to them an evident token of perdition, but to you of salvation, and that of God.***
>
> *Philippians 1:27-28*

## It is the spiritual medicine to our spirit, soul and body

> ***For the word of God is quick, and powerful, and sharper than any twoedged sword, piercing even to the dividing asunder of soul and spirit, and of the joints and marrow, and is a discerner of the thoughts and intents of the heart.***
>
> *Hebrews 4:12*

There is no part of the human body that the Word of God does not have the power to access. It can access your spirit, soul and body to do a perfect work.

## It is God's blessing to mankind

You are blessed as you study the Word and much more as you apply the revelation of the Word to your life daily. You experience a flow of God's blessings as you keep the Word.

> ***But he said, Yea rather, blessed are they that hear the word of God, and keep it.***
>
> *Luke 11:28*

**It accomplishes what it promises**

*(Psalm 33:4; Proverbs 30:5)*

The Word has the capacity to accomplish what it says. God is a Covenant Keeper, as He is not a man to lie. What He says is what He will do.

> ***Heaven and earth shall pass away, but my words shall not pass away.***
>
> *Matthew 24:35*

> ***For as the rain cometh down, and the snow from heaven, and returneth not thither, but watereth the earth, and maketh it bring forth and bud, that it***

> ***may give seed to the sower, and bread to the eater:***
>
> ***So shall my word be that goeth forth out of my mouth: it shall not return unto me void, but it shall accomplish that which I please, and it shall prosper in the thing whereto I sent it.***
>
> *Isaiah 55:10-11*

## It is a spiritual mirror

*(James 1:21-25)*

Nothing can reflect your true position like the Word of God. Looking into the Word of God is like looking into a mirror and seeing your perfect reflection.

## It is a spiritual compass; it shows you the path of life

*(Psalm 16:11)*

The Word of God is a perfect compass that shows you the path of life. You can never go astray following its instructions. God can never mismanage your destiny. So, feel free to trust Him to lead you aright, through His Word.

# 2 Study Methods

***Open thou mine eyes, that I may behold wondrous things out of Thy law.***

*Psalm 119:18*

Reading the Bible is a necessary part of our daily programme. However, it is highly essential to begin by developing an organised plan on how you will approach reading through or studying the Bible for good understanding; otherwise, your effort might be futile.

The Bible, unlike most books, is a compass and you will probably not read it straight from cover to cover. What you desire per time should determine the plan that best suits your purpose.

## Book by Book Study

The Bible is made up of 66 books altogether, from Genesis to Revelation. These books are written by different people. However, the purpose of this method of study is to get the flow, the power and intent of the writer of each book.

You may decide to choose a particular book per time (Matthew, Hebrews, Leviticus, Psalms, etc.) for your study.

Some years ago, my husband took three days off on a mountain, to study only the book of Ezekiel. He had the strangest of encounters there. As he descended from that mountain after three days, the Lord said to him, "Behold I have touched your tongue with the coal of fire and henceforth, as you say it, you will see it." That brought him to a new dimension of signs and wonders in ministry.

With this plan, you are studying the background of the writer, what his relationship with God was and the events at the time of his writing that informed his choice of words. You are equally studying the tone and content of his message, to the people. Finally, you discover how all these apply to your personal life and present situations.

For instance, the books of Jeremiah and Hosea depict graphically the love of God towards man. For Jeremiah, no matter how badly you offend God and how vexed He is in His judgment, He always reserves His love for His people. There will always remain a remnant of His people and for His name's sake, He will always redeem them and punish the nations that oppressed them (Jeremiah 15:1-11, 44:1-30).

You will discover that in all life challenges, there is always a reason to praise God. Dr David Oyedepo says, "If you have lost anything, God is the reason you haven't lost everything; so praise Him!" That is the remnant Jeremiah spoke about. Look hard enough, even in the midst of the most challenging situations of your life, and you will find a reason to keep moving on.

In Hosea, we discover that God's love is eternal. No matter how bad we may think we are or how far we may have gone from God, His love longs after us. Any moment we return to Him, in spite of our filth, with open arms He takes us back and cleans us up once again as if we never sinned. What a love!

This is aptly captured in the story of the prodigal son in Luke 15:10-24. Humanly speaking, that child should not even be allowed to step into the same city as his father. However, by divine principles, his return is worthy of celebration.

Wisdom to handle everyday issues of life is the subject of the book of Proverbs. Wisdom is celebrated as the principal thing upon which every other thing hinges. To get wisdom, study the book of Proverbs.

These are examples of how this method of study helps you to understand God and His ways better, and how you can apply these to your relationships.

### Character Study

The purpose of this study method is to introduce you to the people in the Bible. You will learn about each person's character, accomplishments, strengths and weaknesses, etc. (Abraham – James 2:23, Moses – Hebrews 3:5, David – Acts 13:22, etc). It will also bring you to the understanding of how God interacts with His people, which will aid the application of same to your life, as you study the Bible.

Joseph, for instance, experienced the greatest contradictions in Bible history. God showed him a vision of his glorious destiny. Yet, for over 30 years, he journeyed from the pit, to slavery, then to prison before he ultimately emerged as Prime Minister in a foreign land.

What was his secret? He feared God and believed that no matter how contrary situations might appear, God cannot lie. Whatever He says He will do, will be done. So, he was very infectiously excited, assured that someday his story would change, and it did.

Are you in a contrary situation today? Does it seem like it is taking a long time for God to show up in your situation? Go study the life of Joseph, take the same steps he took and I guarantee you the same results.

### Chapter by Chapter Study

The focus of this kind of study is not in the volume read, but in the depth of understanding of scriptures. This kind of study does not focus on trying to read through the Bible in one year, but being able to track the transformations and testimonies that revelation has generated in your life, in the course of the year.

Each book of the Bible is made up of different number of chapters. For example, the book of Matthew, in the New Testament, is made up of 28 chapters. You may decide to study chapters 1 to 10 only, for a month. In this case, you get to read each chapter at least three times, before the end of that month.

During this period, you are not just reading through but actually studying, taking notes of the revelations you encounter and the application of same to your life. Then take that insight, which should provoke faith in your heart, to God in prayers, until that truth turns you to a living testimony.

Sometimes, you catch a revelation and the Holy Ghost shows you another portion of the Bible that corroborates that revelation, because out of the mouth of two or three witncsses the truth shall be established (2 Corinthians 13:1).

At the end of three months, you should know, like the back of your hands, the revelations you encountered from the book of Matthew. You would know the sequence of events recorded in the book; you would have developed a closer relationship with God and be convinced beyond any doubt that the miracles recorded therein can be reproduced several times. This is because you would have encountered some of them, as you prayed in faith, provoked by the encounters with the Word.

It is wisdom to study the Bible in this order or at least once a year. That way, you don't assume a parable or story just because it seems vague. Also, it helps you to avoid interpreting the Scripture out of context or in your own way, which is where misunderstandings often come in (2 Peter 1:20-21).

## Reading Through

You can develop a plan on how to read through the Bible on your own. For instance, you can decide to read through the Old Testament at least once a year. As you read, ensure that you take note of any truth you want to remember.

Anything you do not immediately understand or questions that come to your mind that you do not immediately find answers to, can become the starting point for more in-depth study using concordance, commentaries and other reference tools or books.

For the New Testament, you can follow a different plan. Similar to the chapter by chapter study, you can decide to read one book at a time repeatedly, for a month or more. As you study, try to memorise any particular verse(s) that ministers the most to you that day. That will help you to retain some of the scriptures, so that you won't always have to depend on a concordance to find them.

You can begin with a very short book like Jude, Philemon or better still 1 John, 2 John or 3 John for a good understanding of the love of God. Read it through in one sitting, every day, for 30 days. Write down in your note the major theme of each chapter.

As you study and look through your notes daily, you will begin to remember the content of each chapter and develop a perception of the book with your mind's eye. By so doing, at the end of your study, you will have a good knowledge of the book.

With longer books, you can divide them into smaller sections and read each section daily for 30 days. For instance, the book of John contains 21 chapters. You can divide it into three sections of seven chapters each. At the end of 90 days, you would have finished the book.

For variety, you could alternate between short and long books. In less than three years, you would have finished the entire New Testament and would really know it.

You could also decide to read one out of the 31 chapters of the book of Proverbs and three out of the 150 chapters of the book of Psalms every day. Every month, you would have read through both books completely. You can decide to do that for the whole year and during each study, you will discover greater insights even from the same scriptures you studied previously.

## Topical Study

This is very different from every other method of study. Here, you pick a particular topic of interest for your study per time. This will give you a clear and perfect understanding of those scriptures you have heard over time, and perhaps, which have not really made so much meaning to you. Scanning through subject indexes of the Bible (though not all Bibles have this), you definitely will find some topics such as salvation, obedience, sin, prosperity, healing, etc., that will interest you.

For instance, if you have a health

challenge, it wouldn't be wise to set a target to read through the Bible in one year. What you need is healing. So, looking through the index of your Bible, prayerfully search for every chapter and verse that has to do with healing.

Study each verse prayerfully; you could even write out the verses, paste them around you and keep reading them, sometimes aloud to yourself, until the truths embedded in those verses are fully assimilated.

Again, in this type of study, it is not in the volume but in the depth of understanding. In which case, you can take just a few verses of the Bible relating to your area of challenge and meditate on them, until the truth delivers your desires into your hands.

## The Use of Study Guide

Various study guide materials are available these days. They are usually packaged on a yearly Bible reading plan. In most cases, the contents are divided into days, weeks, months, etc., with scriptural references and brief explanations. You can take advantage of such for your edification.

One or a combination of two or more of the above will help you, a great deal, to effectively enjoy the "juice" of the Word!

In addition, each book of the Bible has great introductions which could give you a good background understanding.

Each page of the Bible has a specific topic at the top (though not all Bibles have this). This topic gives an insight to the content of that page. Always read and ponder on them, as they can be very helpful during your study.

Personally, I read them thoughtfully and it has been a very great eye-opening experience for me.

# 3 Study Tools

***And the LORD said unto him, What is that in thine hand? And he said, A rod.***

*Exodus 4:2*

Tools are important and helpful items that can be used to achieve a goal. However, reading and studying the Bible are the most important in spiritual development.

Therefore, the following study tools are meant to simplify the process of Bible study, so as to make the most of your study time.

The most important tool is, **a complete Holy Bible** (one that has both Old & New Testaments). Getting a Bible that has different translations can enhance very good understanding. If you cannot find one, you can buy two or more Bibles of different versions.

For instance, in addition to having a King James or New King James version of the Bible, you could also get The Living Bible (particularly if you are just starting out in Bible study) or the Amplified version. So, if you read a chapter in the King James Version, you could read that same chapter in the Living or Amplified versions of the Bible to give you a clearer understanding of that chapter.

## Concordance

Concordance is an essential tool for studying God's Word. It is required to help you look up some root words and see how they are translated in other places in the Bible. This ultimately enhances your level of understanding of God's Word. It also makes cross-referencing easier.

## Writing materials such as notebook, pen, etc.

During your studies, you will discover new ideas, encounter insights and revelations. If not written down in your note, they might be forgotten.

This is why you must cultivate the habit of writing down insights and revelations. Statistically, it is said that you will remember some percentage of what you read, but you will most likely remember much more of what you write. Also, you can always refer to what is written, to refresh your memory.

### Other Relevant Materials

Publications such as anointed books, tracts, magazines, etc., can be invaluable assets in your study. Particularly for subject study, you will need books by anointed authors; they make your search so much easier.

At a time, my husband, Bishop David Oyedepo, took his Bible, jotter, two books on prosperity, and locked himself in a room for three days. While reading one of the books, he discovered that prosperity is a covenant.

The Holy Spirit directed him to read Deuteronomy 8:18 as a confirmation, and told him that prosperity has no respect for prayer or fasting, but only for the practice of the covenant. So, he screamed, "I can never be poor!"

That singular revelation and the consistent practice of that covenant have brought him and multitudes of people out of poverty into Kingdom prosperity today.

In this age of technology, electronic materials such as audio and video CDs, audio books, e-books, teaching tapes, Christian blogs on social media, etc., are very resourceful materials that will greatly aid you in your study.

They help, a great deal, to shed more light on what is already written in the

Word, which automatically aids your understanding of God's Word on every issue of concern.

# 4 Study Steps

***...precept must be upon precept, precept upon precept, Line upon line, line upon line, Here a little, there a little.***

*Isaiah 28:10 (NKJV)*

You learn the Word of God precept by precept per time. The word "precept", as defined by the Dictionary, is *a commandment or direction given as a rule of action or conduct.* Learning God's precepts one at a time and faithfully living in line with each precept or commandment, will help you to grow in the things of God and get you ready for more advanced revelations.

You may ask, "Is there any difference between reading and studying the Bible?" Undoubtedly, there is a world of difference between the two.

Just anybody can pick up the Bible to read, which could be done obligatorily, religiously, scientifically, cynically, etc. But, studying the Word of God is only done by those who seek to have the Word in their hearts, in order to generate a desired change (Psalm 119:11). "Reading" enforces no personal application, but studying implies that the words are pondered on and purposely applied.

As you study, ask yourself the question: How does this Word apply to my life? Intermittently, stop to ponder over the verses you have read, praying for understanding as you think about what they mean. As you ask questions in your mind, wait for spiritual understanding and write down revelations and insights as they come to your mind. This way, you can remember them and be able to refer to them at some other time.

You can read your Bible without writing something down. But, you can't study without having something to write down. Dawson Trotman said, "Thoughts disentangle themselves when they pass through the lips and fingertips." In other words, unless you are able to say it or write it down, you have not really thought about it.

Studying is not so much about the volume or chapters you read per time;

although setting targets for yourself is essential. It is much more about how much of the Word studied you understand.

The following are a few steps to effectively give yourself to the study of the Word:

**Prepare Your Heart**

*(Proverbs 16:1)*

This is very crucial to effective Word study. Sanitise your heart from every form of spiritual blockage such as sin, anger, bitterness – all the "little foxes" in your life that are likely to hinder your access to being enlightened and receiving revelation during your study.

Ask God, in a very simple prayer, to help you understand the scriptures as you study (Luke 24:45; Acts 16:14).

Prayer is how we communicate with God, and studying His Word is how He communicates with us. So, asking for His help by the Holy Spirit makes His communication with you very easy.

## Have a Purpose

*(Proverbs 18:1)*

To start off meaningfully, you can select a purpose or topic to study. For instance, what do you want to know or learn about? What area of life are you struggling with or what Godly principle would you want to improve upon?

Search through the topics behind your Bible, look up and read all the scriptures that refer to that topic. Writing down all or part of a verse of scripture can help you to fully ponder more on its meaning and how you can apply it to your life.

**Purposely Set Aside Time**
*(Ecclesiastes 3:1)*

Make an appointment with God from His Word, at a scheduled time, every day. It could be anytime of the day – morning, afternoon, evening or at night. Most importantly, it should be a time that would be convenient for you personally to assimilate.

Personally, early in the morning and night time have been most helpful study times for me. However, the length of time shouldn't be an issue, but must be reasonably long enough, to capture what God is communicating to you.

Jesus, speaking to His disciples, said:

***...could ye not watch... one hour?***

*Matthew 26:40*

Putting forth real effort, just start somewhere and you will see the fruit that this time brings to your life. However, it is highly recommended as you get into the habit, to target at least 30 minutes to an hour, to feed on the Word of God for maximum impact on your life and destiny, regularly.

### Seek for a Conducive Place
(*Genesis 28:12-17*)

There is definitely a place of encounter for you, and you have to locate the place. It could be a room in your house where you can be alone or somewhere you are comfortable with and like to be.

However, it is important that you

choose a conducive and quiet place where you will not be interrupted or disturbed – that is, somewhere comfortable for efficient study. There should be a reading table and chair in that place, to be able to write if you need to. It is also important that wherever you decide to use be well illuminated to help you stay alert.

**Get all your study tools available**
*(Hosea 10:12)*

Ensure you make adequate preparation; this implies having all your study tools such as a complete Bible, concordance, dictionary and writing materials before you start studying. This is to ensure that there is no break in-between your study, in search of one or two things.

## Expect an Encounter
(*Proverbs 23:18*)

Expectation is the mother of manifestation. What you do not expect, you cannot manifest. Therefore, desire an encounter while studying God's Word. An encounter could also be referred to as revelation – light from God's Word on any area of concern in your life. You must expect God to speak to you during your study.

Remember to pray before you start and at intervals as you read (Psalm 119:18). Read your designated passage(s) more than once (Isaiah 34:16); pause, meditate, reference relevant scriptures, etc., (Joshua 1:8; 1 Timothy 4:13-15). You should also write or document as you study (Isaiah 30:8; Jeremiah 30:2).

## Be consistent and don't give up
*(Isaiah 26:9)*

Finally, as you study the Bible daily, don't give up or be discouraged, but follow through with diligence. Human nature wants everything to be delivered easily. If you will humble yourself daily before the Lord, studying the Word as if your daily existence depends on it, asking God to reveal Himself to you in a new and living way, your life will be greatly transformed and your attitude to the Word of God will be amazing.

Studying God's Word will change your life; but it starts with a willingness to study. God has so much He wants to show you, but you must first be willing to look into His Word.

***Open thou mine eyes, that I may***

***behold wondrous things out of Thy law.***

*Psalm 119:18*

Approach your study times with a sense of devotion. While studying the Word, do not be particular about reciting or memorising the verses; purposefully look out for a revelation of Jesus and the effect of His death and resurrection in reconciling humanity to God.

Your ability to understand the Word of God will greatly increase, as you employ this pattern of study and apply the revelation of the Word to your personal life.

# 5 Benefits of Studying The Bible

***Study to shew thyself approved unto God, a workman that needeth not to be ashamed, rightly dividing the word of truth.***

*2 Timothy 2:15*

It is important to note that there is a world of difference between Bible reading and Bible study. When you read, you only have access to the letters of the Word, but when you study, you have access to the depth therein. Understanding the true meaning of what you have read is dependent upon effective study, not mere reading.

An effective Bible study requires a systematic and comprehensive programme of scriptural study that leads to a clearer understanding of God's Word – the Holy Bible. Studying gives you a clearer understanding of God's nature, the person of Jesus Christ, the work of the Holy Spirit, the gift of salvation and the hope of an eternal life with God.

Studying the Bible is vital because as it is clearly stated, it is ***...profitable for doctrine, for reproof, for correction, for instruction in righteousness*** (2 Timothy 3:16).

Word study will give you daily guidance, direction and clarity of purpose in life (Psalm 119:105).

Also, God clearly commanded us to study, in order not to experience shame (2 Timothy 2:15). In the world today, where people decide what they want to believe and then choose the verses of scriptures that support their belief, while ignoring the verses that seemingly contradict that belief, it is important you personally understand the Scripture.

Today, men under satanic influence interpret the Bible according to what they want. This leads to confusion and a lot of doctrinal differences, even within the same Christian faith.

As stated in Ephesians 4:4-6 and 1 Corinthians 14:33, there is only one Spirit, one faith and one God, Who is not the author of confusion. The doctrinal differences in Christendom today, are glaring examples of why it is absolutely necessary to personally study the Bible.

It doesn't matter what you are told from the pulpit, the only important thing is God's Word as recorded in your Bible. Recognise that by it, you will be judged when you ultimately stand before God and not according to man's interpretations or misinterpretations of it.

That you lived faithfully according to what you were taught will not matter, if it differs from what the Bible says. The only source of truth is the Word (John 17:17). That is why you must study it to show yourself approved unto God as a workman that needeth not to be ashamed. Therefore, to avoid error and false teaching, study the Bible for yourself (1 Timothy 4:16; Hosea 4:6; Galatians 1:8-9).

God has given us what is required to discern what is necessary for salvation and righteousness via His Word and the guidance of the Holy Spirit. The Word gives power to overcome sin (Psalm 119:11). It is a weapon against temptation (Matthew 4:3-4).

Jesus was tempted of the devil, just as we all are today and His weapon of victory was the Word of God. He kept declaring to the devil what was written. When the devil misrepresented the Word, His (Jesus) depth of understanding made Him to know it was a wrong interpretation. So, He declared the correct interpretation and triumphed.

> ***And he brought him to Jerusalem, and set him on a pinnacle of the temple, and said unto him, If thou be the Son of God, cast thyself down from hence:***
>
> ***For it is written, He shall give his angels charge over thee, to keep thee:***
>
> ***And in their hands they shall bear thee up, lest at any time thou dash thy foot against a stone.***
>
> ***And Jesus answering said unto him, It is said, Thou shalt not tempt the Lord thy God.***
>
> *Luke 4:9-12*

Moreover, everyone that seeks is entitled to find answers in the Word, to every question of life (Matthew 7:7, 4:1-11). Therefore, no one has any excuse for living below what the Word offers.

What breathing, eating and drinking is to your physical body, is what daily intake of the Word of God is to your soul. To see growth and development, that is, spiritual maturity in your spiritual walk with God, you must develop your faith level. That comes as you continuously take in the Word of God daily. The faith that works comes from hearing the Word of God (Romans 10:17).

Life will be void of colour and dignity, if it is not lived victoriously. Note that an effective study of the Word is the master key to a victorious life (Ephesians 6:17). Paul, the great Apostle of our Lord Jesus Christ, made it clear that within the gospel resides the great power of God. He said:

> ***For I am not ashamed of the gospel of Christ: for it is the power of God unto***

***salvation to every one that believeth...***

*Romans 1:16*

If you must encounter the empowerment required for a victorious Christian life, then you must generate it from the Word of God. The Word has all you require to enjoy freedom in any area of life. Often times, the devil subjects you to bondage of guilt because of past mistakes. However, the Word has the power to deliver you from past pains, guilt and bad habits (John 8:31-32). When you know the truth of God's love via His Word, you shall be set free indeed.

A brother was addicted to smoking. Even though he knew the habit would send him to an early grave, he couldn't stop. He did all he could, but there was no change. One day, he decided to study one of Dr. David Oyedepo's books titled, *The Blood Triumph.* From the book, he got an understanding of the power in the Blood of Jesus. He appropriated that power and was instantly delivered from that hold of hell over his life. Today, the knowledge of the truth discovered, while he studied, set him free.

May the benefits of studying the Bible be made manifest in your life more than ever!

# 6 Covenant Platforms

***Through desire a man, having separated himself, seeketh and intermeddleth with all wisdom.***

*Proverbs 18:1*

A productive study of the Word of God demands some level of preparation on your part, which is referred to in this book as Covenant Platforms. They are:

**Salvation**

While non-Christians can garner surface biblical knowledge, they are not capable of accessing full spiritual meaning of the Scripture. The Bible says in 1 Corinthians 2:14:

> ***But the natural man receiveth not the things of the Spirit of God: for they are foolishness unto him: neither can he know them, because they are spiritually discerned.***

The only way to truly understand the Bible is to be taught by the Holy Spirit for ***...no one knows the things of God except the Spirit of God*** (1 Corinthians 2:11 paraphrased) and that is only possible for those who are born-again (1 John 2:27).

Harbouring sin in your life will lead you to misinterpret scriptures to fit your lifestyle or make you avoid the Word in whole or in part. You cannot be an honest and effective student of God's Word, with sin in your life.

> ***Wherefore lay apart all filthiness and superfluity of naughtiness, and receive with meekness the engrafted word, which is able to save your souls.***
>
> *James 1:21*

In case you have not given your life to Christ by verbally inviting Him into your heart to be your Lord and Saviour, or perhaps you were once born again but you fell into sin and you would want to reconnect to Him, please turn to the last page of this book right now and pray the sinner's prayer audibly. The God of mercy is always ready to receive you, as you reconcile with Him.

## Desire

*(Proverbs 2:3-5; Matthew 5:6; Jeremiah 29:13)*

Your desire for the Word will be evident in your love, passion, honour and respect for the Word of God. You will desire more and more of the Word, just as new born babes desire milk (1 Peter 2:2).

Your desire must reflect in your thirst, because only those who are thirsty shall be filled (Matthew 5:6).

> ***Ho, every one that thirsteth, come ye to the waters, and he that hath no money; come ye, buy, and eat; yea, come, buy wine and milk without money and without price.***
>
> ***Wherefore do ye spend money for that which is not bread? and your labour for that which satisfieth not? hearken***

***diligently unto me, and eat ye that which is good, and let your soul delight itself in fatness.***

*Isaiah 55:1-2*

## Separation
*(Romans 1:1)*

You have to dedicate a special place in your home for study. Find yourself a "study nook" and make it your special place of encounter with God in His Word. It should be where you enjoy staying and visiting almost every day.

I have found in my own personal experience that very early in the morning or late at night is the best time to separate yourself to study the Word. It is devoid of distraction and you can give yourself absolutely to what you are doing.

## Diligence

*(Proverbs 14:23, 21:5)*

Diligence requires that you give more than just a daily devotion to the Word. You are to labour in the Word, to be approved as a workman that will not be ashamed (2 Timothy 2:15). You are expected to search the Scripture daily, giving due diligence to make your calling and election sure (2 Peter 1:10).

## Faith

*(Matthew 21:22; Romans 14:23; Philemon 1:6)*

It is important you approach God's Word with faith that you will find Him as you seek Him via His Word. Your encounter will not be complete if you do not have faith in God, because as far as He is concerned ***...whatsoever is not***

***of faith is sin*** (Romans 14:23).

Faith is the key to a victorious Christian life, and it is the basis of any meaningful relationship with God and His Word.

# 7 The Place of Prayer and Fasting

***Howbeit this kind goeth not out but by prayer and fasting.***

*Matthew 17:21*

Prayer and fasting are non-negotiable requirements for access to revelation, which comes principally from Word study.

### Prayer and Word Study

*(Psalm 119:18)*

Clearly, it is essential to study the Bible prayerfully. This could be said to be the first step in understanding the Bible.

Word study should be approached with a prayerful desire to learn (Psalm 86:11). After all, it is spiritual food (Jeremiah 15:16; 1 Peter 2:2).

God Himself is the Word and also the Author of the Word (John 1:1-4). Therefore, there cannot be an effective study of the Word without involving the Initiator. He alone can best interpret His Word to your understanding, if you invite Him in prayer.

### Fasting and Word Study

*(Isaiah 58:1-9)*

True fasting can be defined as voluntarily going without food, in order to focus on a spiritual exercise. **It is resisting and fleeing from selfish desires.** It is not about avoiding physical food while indulging one's greed and selfishness, but ***to loose the bands of wickedness, to undo the heavy burdens, and to let the oppressed go free*** (Isaiah 58:1–9).

However, fasting without prayer equals starvation (Matthew 6:16). That is why it is highly beneficial to maximise your fasting period in prayer and Word study.

### Prayer, Fasting & Word Study
*(Matthew 6:16-18)*

In this context, having a dedicated time of prayer and fasting is not a way of manipulating God to do what you desire. It is simply compelling yourself to focus and rely on God for the strength, provision, and wisdom you need from His Word through meditation (Hebrews 5:13-14; 1 Kings 19:7-15; John 4:32-34).

The place of prayer and fasting cannot be overemphasised in effectual study of the Word. So, when you go to God in prayer backed up with fasting, He opens your eyes of understanding to the mystery behind the letters that you may never have thought of.

Prayer and fasting are essential factors for building a real relationship with God through His Word. By taking our eyes off the things of this world through prayer and fasting, we can focus better on Christ (Matthew 6:16-18).

It is, therefore, expedient for you to spend time fasting and praying, in order to gain a deeper fellowship with God through His Word.

It is not enough to fast and pray; it is also important to expect definite encounters from the Word, while studying. The Interpreter (the Holy Spirit) is ever present to grant your heart's desires, as you engage prayerfully in that study.

Supplication and revelation go hand in hand.

> ***Praying always with all prayer and supplication in the Spirit, and watching thereunto with all perseverance and supplication for all saints;***
>
> *Ephesians 6:18*

As you pray, the Holy Ghost unveils some revelations of His Word that are answers to certain issues in your life.

Fasting causes your light (revelation) to break forth.

> ***Is not this the fast that I have chosen...? Then shall thy light break***

***forth as the morning...***

*Isaiah 58:6-8*

Prayer and fasting boosts your access to revelation, when you study God's Word. With your heart devoid of distractions as you fast, access to revelation becomes very easy.

Therefore, expect a free flow of revelation that proffers solutions to the issues of your life, as you study the Word when you fast and pray.

# 8

# The Principal Teacher: The Holy Spirit

***For the Holy Spirit will teach you...***

*Luke 12:12 (NIV)*

***But ...the Holy Spirit ...will teach you all things...***

*John 14:26 (NIV)*

The Holy Spirit is our Principal Teacher in accessing the deep things of God (John 16:13; 1 Corinthians 2:9-10). Jesus promised to send us the Holy Spirit, Who would teach us all things. There is no better way to understand the Scripture than having the Writer reveal to you what He means by what He wrote.

It is impossible to understand the Word, without the Holy Spirit giving you understanding.

There is a vivid encounter recorded in Acts 8:30-36 on this point:

> ***And Philip ran thither to him, and heard him read the prophet Esaias, and said, Understandest thou what thou readest?***
>
> ***And he said, How can I, except some man should guide me? And he desired Philip that he would come up and sit with him.***
>
> ***The place of the scripture which he read was this, He was led as a sheep to the slaughter; and like a lamb dumb before his shearer, so opened he not his mouth:***
>
> ***In his humiliation his judgment was***

> ***taken away: and who shall declare his generation? for his life is taken from the earth.***
>
> ***And the eunuch answered Philip, and said, I pray thee, of whom speaketh the prophet this? of himself, or of some other man?***
>
> ***Then Philip opened his mouth, and began at the same scripture, and preached unto him Jesus.***
>
> ***And as they went on their way, they came unto a certain water: and the eunuch said, See, here is water; what doth hinder me to be baptized?***

For maximum study you will need to:

### Interpret the Word

Always seek an interpretation of what you are studying. Learn to ask questions as you study, such as: What does this mean? What do I understand by what I have read thus far? Look up words from the concordance, cross references and ask the Holy Ghost, in just a few words of prayer, to help you interpret the Word as you study.

### Evaluate the Revelation

It is essential to appraise the truth of what you are studying. To ensure you do not misinterpret the Word, you need to do some appraisal of the Word. The Bible says in Matthew 18:16:

> ***...that in the mouth of two or three witnesses every word may be established.***

The Bible will never contradict itself. So, if you encounter a revelation that has no cross-reference, be careful because sometimes, the devil even presents himself as an angel of light with intent to deceive you (2 Corinthians 11:14).

There is nothing new under the sun. Therefore, when you have a revelation, check other sources like anointed books on the subject. You will definitely find someone who had the same revelation, sometimes, even from another passage of the Scripture.

### Apply the Principles

In John 13:17, Jesus said: ***If ye know these things, happy are ye if ye do them.*** In other words, it is not just enough to know the truth. The joy it brings is only deliverable as you apply that truth to your life, by taking steps in line with the revelation.

> ***As newborn babes, desire the sincere milk of the word, that ye***

***may grow thereby:***

*1 Peter 2:2*

Growth is the ultimate purpose of the Word of God. As with the physical body, having food on your table without eating it holds no profit for your nourishment and growth; the same is true of your spiritual growth. You will never grow beyond the level of your application of revelation.

For instance, you discover the truth that the key to prosperity is the practice of the covenant, which is the law of seedtime and harvest (Genesis 8:22). Rather than sow the seed that will bring you harvest, you decide to confess on a daily basis, "God gives me power to get wealth" (Deuteronomy 8:18); you will never "taste" prosperity.

As you study, ask yourself, "How does

this revelation apply to me? What changes is it designed to bring about in my life? Is there a promise in it that I can plug myself into by practice?" As you take steps to apply the Word, you will see positive growth and development in your spiritual life and experience.

As someone said, "If there is a command to be obeyed, obey it. If there is a promise to be embraced, claim it. If there is a warning to be followed, heed it." This is the ultimate – apply the Word of God and let it transform you.

### Correlate the Truth

You should be able to link one revelation with another from different parts of the Bible. For instance, I saw in Psalm 46:10, **"Be still, and know that I am God..."**, at a time when it was like the battles of life were about to consume me. It seemed ridiculous to be still at a time like that. Then I saw from 2 Chronicles 20:17,

> ***Ye shall not need to fight in this battle: set yourselves, stand ye still, and see the salvation of the LORD with you...***

That gave me rest and glory to God, the battle was won!

All of these come by the teaching ministry of the Holy Spirit. The question then is:

## How do you enjoy the teaching ministry of the Holy Spirit?

### Acknowledge His person

*(John 14:16-17)*

The Holy Spirit is the third person of the God-head. You must recognise Him as the Comforter whom Jesus promised to send unto us when He said:

> ***Nevertheless I tell you the truth; It is expedient for you that I go away: for if I go not away, the Comforter will not come unto you; but if I depart, I will send him unto you.***
>
> *John 16:7*

**Believe in His teaching ministry**

The Holy Ghost is sent to teach us all things. But it will take you believing in His teaching ministry to enjoy Him.

> ***But the anointing which ye have received of him abideth in you, and ye need not that any man teach you: but as the same anointing teacheth you of all things...***
>
> *1 John 2:27*

## Receive Him as your teacher

He is a gentle Spirit waiting to be invited to teach. Until you receive Him as your teacher and be ready to allow Him teach you, He will not. See Him the way you see your secular teachers. You neither interrupt any teaching class nor argue with your teachers.

Most often, you believe that whatever your teacher says is the absolute truth. Likewise, allow the Holy Spirit to teach you without doubting.

> ***But the Comforter, which is the Holy Ghost, whom the Father will send in my name, he shall teach you all things, and bring all things to your remembrance, whatsoever I have said unto you.***
>
> *John 14:26*

## Desire/Ask Him to teach you

A fundamental requirement for the realisation of any promise by God is the need to ask. Until you ask, even though God knows you have a need in any area, He is not committed to give it to you.

> ***Ask, and it shall be given you; seek, and ye shall find; knock, and it shall be opened unto you:***
>
> ***For every one that asketh receiveth; and he that seeketh findeth; and to him that knocketh it shall be opened.***
>
> *Mathew 7:7-8*

You must ask the Holy Spirit to teach you what you do not know.

## Develop an intimate relationship with Him

You cannot enjoy the ministry of your Teacher without being in an intimate relationship with Him, which implies being baptised in the Holy Spirit, with the evidence of speaking in tongues.

For example, Apostle Paul was full of abundance of revelation (1 Corinthians 12:7), yet he testified:

> ***I thank my God, I speak with tongues more than ye all.***
>
> *1 Corinthians 14:18*

## Steps to Receiving the Baptism of the Holy Ghost

### Be born again

*(Acts 2:38-39; John 2:2-3)*

The baptism of the Holy Spirit involves both the Holy Spirit and Jesus Christ, the Baptiser. Therefore, the baptism is preceded by a total surrender and absolute commitment to the Lordship of Jesus Christ; that is, accepting Him as your Lord and personal Saviour.

You cannot be baptised until you first repent of your sins and become His disciple. That is the major prerequisite.

> ***Then Peter said unto them, Repent, and be baptized every one of you in the name of Jesus Christ for the remission of sins, and ye shall receive the gift of the Holy Ghost.***
>
> ***For the promise is unto you, and to your children, and to all that are afar off, even as many as the Lord our God shall call.***
>
> *Acts 2:38-39*

### Desire to be baptised

*(Isaiah 55:1)*

The baptism of the Holy Ghost is available to anyone who thirsts for it. You must desire to live a life that is pleasing to the Lord. The Bible gives you a definite assurance in Matthew 5:6, which says:

> ***Blessed are they which do hunger and thirst after righteousness: for they shall be filled.***

The Holy Spirit will gladly fill you up, if your sincere desire is to be controlled and empowered by Him.

### Ask Jesus Christ to baptise you
*(Matthew 7:7; Luke 11:13)*

It is important that you verbally ask Jesus to baptise you with the Holy Spirit. God gave the command in Ephesians 5:18: ***And be not drunk with wine, wherein is excess; but be filled with the Spirit;*** and He is committed to fulfilling His Word when you ask

Him.

Being filled is a command and a promise. In Acts 1:4-5, Jesus said:

> ***...being assembled together with them, commanded them that they should not depart from Jerusalem, but wait for the promise of the Father, which, saith he, ye have heard of me.***
>
> ***For John truly baptized with water; but ye shall be baptized with the Holy Ghost not many days hence.***

It is this promise that makes the command possible, because we have this assurance in approaching God that if we ask anything according to His will, He hears us. And if we know that He hears us, then we know that we automatically have what we ask of Him.

## Believe that you have received in faith

*(Mark 11:24)*

It is important to note that anything you desire from God can only be given on the platform of faith, and this includes baptism of the Holy Ghost. Jesus said in Luke 11:13:

> ***If ye then, being evil, know how to give good gifts unto your children: how much more shall your heavenly Father give the Holy Spirit to them that ask him?***

When you ask in faith, the Holy Spirit comes to live in you and when you are filled, the first proof is that you begin to speak in tongues.

## Expect the Holy Ghost to give you utterance

You must expect the Holy Spirit to put

supernatural words (tongues) into your spirit, and also move upon your vocal cords. The Lord will not force you to speak in tongues. He will give you the utterance, but you have to do the speaking.

> ***And they were all filled with the Holy Ghost, and began to speak with other tongues, as the Spirit gave them utterance.***
>
> *Acts 2:4*

## Yield your tongue/Begin to speak by faith

*(Acts 2:4)*

Understand that the moment you ask, God baptises and fills you with the Holy Spirit. What you must do is to willingly yield your tongue to speak. You don't need to beg for it or try to understand the words you are saying,

> ***For he that speaketh in an unknown tongue speaketh not unto men, but unto God: for no man understandeth him; howbeit in the spirit he speaketh mysteries.***
>
> *1 Corinthians 14:2*

God's Word says:

> ***...how much more shall your heavenly Father give the Holy Spirit to them that ask him?***
>
> *Luke 11:13*

Thus, if you desire to be baptised in the Holy Ghost, you can ask Him right now by praying with faith in your heart saying:

*Dear God, I desire the baptism of the Holy Spirit. Your Word says if I ask, I will receive. I believe with all my heart that Your Word is true. Therefore, I ask that You fill me to overflowing with Your precious Holy Spirit, in the name of Jesus Christ. I also believe that Jesus is the Baptiser, as I was told. Therefore, baptise me in the Holy Spirit, now!*

*Thank You Jesus, for by faith, I receive and believe that I now have the Holy Spirit right inside me. Holy Spirit, I fully expect to speak with other tongues, as You give me the utterance, in Jesus' name I pray. Amen!*

You can now begin to give voice to the expressions in your heart; yield your tongue and speak by faith. Congratulations! You have just been baptised in the Holy Spirit.

# 9

# Maximising the Benefits of the Word

***If ye know these things, happy are ye if ye do them.***

*John 13:17*

## Let the Word of God dwell richly in you

*(Colossians 3:16)*

Bear in mind that Jesus Christ Himself is the Word. However, before the Word can profit you, it must first enter into you. That is, unless you read and hear it, you will not know what is embedded in it for your benefit.

It is also important that you don't just stop at reading and hearing the Word, but you go a step further by making it a way of life. This means, you should let God's Word seep through you into your innermost being. Once the Word gains access into your heart, it will purify, clean and change you further into Christ's likeness.

Nevertheless, this is not a once-in-a-lifetime exercise. For the Word to *dwell* richly in you, it must *remain* in your heart, forever. That way, you constantly exhibit the nature of Christ in all you do, thereby turning you to a living wonder among men.

**Meditation**

*(Joshua 1:8)*

Meditation is a spiritual process done in partnership with the Holy Spirit. So, you need patience, waiting on Him, sensitivity and open-mindedness.

Through the process of meditation, the Holy Spirit reveals to you the hidden picture in every scripture, and this will help you to maximise the benefits of the Word. You can't see a picture from a scripture and doubt it (1 Corinthians 2:9-11).

It is the process of scriptural meditation that kills doubts and unbelief (Hebrews 3:12). It empowers you to believe, which automatically leads to FAITH.

It helps you to enter into God's rest on any issue of concern (Hebrews 4:3, 11). It also helps you to access revelation that destroys frustration and doubt.

It helps you to trust God and be God-confident, because of the revelation shown to you by the Holy Spirit (Daniel 11:32). Studying God's Word builds faith and faith builds trust.

Simply put, to live a successful and prosperous life as a believer, you need to practise the art of meditation often and make it your lifestyle (John 15:7).

For example, the Bible records concerning Isaac:

> ***And Isaac went out to meditate in the field at the eventide: and he lifted up his eyes, and saw, and, behold, the camels were coming.***
>
> *Genesis 24:63*

## Bold Speaking

*(Acts 4:23-31)*

The scriptural reference above gives us several examples of both bold living and bold speaking. Bold speaking means courage to speak openly with assurance and confidence, and to act without fear.

As an ambassador of Christ, you need boldness to live a triumphant life in this world. However, bold speaking is largely influenced by what you believe deeply. You can only be empowered to believe what you see from God's Word, which is also referred to as revelation.

Bold speaking can be done through: *Speaking boldly to ourselves (1 Samuel 30:6), Speaking encouragement to others (Hebrews 3:13), Speaking correction to others (Hebrews 12:5-11) and leading others to Christ (Acts 4:20).*

Learn to boldly speak God's Word.

### Obedience

*(John 2:5; James 1:22-25)*

It is your main duty, as a believer, to obey God and His Word. However, obedience goes deeper than just a duty. It must come from the heart, not grudgingly, but because we have to.

What you know is not as important as what you do with what you know.

Your obedience is an expression of your faith in God's wisdom and love. When you obey God's Word, you have obeyed His person as well. Note that as your Creator, He has the wisdom to know how you should live and what works best for you in the long run.

It is, therefore, essential to trust God because His perspective is much better than yours, as seen in His Word (Isaiah 55:8-9).

Remember, what you do with God's Word determines your worth in this world.

# SALVATION PRAYER

All that is written in this book can only work for children of God. That is, those who have given their lives to Jesus and accepted Him as their Lord and personal Saviour. If you have not, you too can be a part of these blessed people, who are united with Him through His Blood and Flesh. All you need is to realise that:

* All have sinned and come short of the glory of God, yourself inclusive (Romans 3:23).
* Sin has separated you from God (Isaiah 59:2).
* God has made provision for you to be reunited with Him (John 6:37).
* The provision He made was to send His Son Jesus Christ to die for you (John 3:16).

The only condition God places before you to becoming His child is to accept Jesus Christ as your Lord and personal Saviour (Romans 10:10). Having considered this truth, you can say this prayer aloud:

***Father, I realise that I have been a sinner. Today, I come before You asking for forgiveness of my sins. I believe in the death and resurrection of Jesus Christ and I believe in His power to save me, if I ask Him to. Save me and accept me as Your son/daughter. Write my name in the Book of Life. Thank You Father for saving me, in Jesus' Name, Amen.***

# ABOUT THE *Author*

Faith Abiola Oyedepo has, through the leading of the Holy Spirit, brought hope, joy and peace into many families and homes.

For many years since she received the ministry for families and homes, she has in no little measure dedicated her life to showing people the perfect will of God concerning their family relationships and homes. Her regular and scintillating weekly newspaper and internet columns - Family Matters, Family Success and Family Life, among others - have helped in no small measure in achieving this goal.

Also, she has a divine mandate to enrich the lives of singles and unmarried persons in a unique way.

She reaches out to the less privileged, the needy and those in the valley of decision, through her Faith Abiola Oyedepo Foundation (FAOF).

Pastor Faith has written over 20 anointed and impactful books that have transformed many lives and given them change of stories, including her best-selling title: *Rescued From Destruction.*

An anointed preacher of the Gospel, Pastor Faith has been doggedly supportive of her husband (Dr David O. Oyedepo, the Visionary/President Of Living Faith Church Worldwide Inc.) in the work of the ministry. They are parents to four children – David Jnr., Isaac, Love and Joys.

# Books By Faith Oyedepo

- Arise And Be Healed
- Holy Ghost: Your Helper
- The Force Of Joy
- The Force Of Hope
- Building A Successful Family
- Making Marriage Work
- Success In Marriage *(Co-authored with Dr David Oyedepo)*
- Marriage Covenant
- Raising Godly Children
- Rescued From Destruction
- Single With A Difference
- The Effective Minister's Wife
- The Spirit Of Faith
- A Living Witness *(Expanded version)*
- Nurturing The Incorruptible Seed *(Expanded version)*
- Service: The Master Key *(Expanded version)*
- The Dignity Of The Believer *(Expanded version)*
- Growing In Grace
- The Power Of The Communion Table
- Healing, Health And Wholeness
- Overcoming Anxiety
- Salvation: The Way Of Escape
- The Healing Scriptures
- The Healing Ministry Of Jesus Christ
- You Are Welcome To God's Family
- Understanding Motherhood